CREATING ACTIVITIES
FOR
DIFFERENT LEARNER TYPES

A Guide for ELT Teachers, Trainers, and Writers

Marjorie Rosenberg

WAYZGOOSE PRESS

Creating Activities for Different Learner Types
Copyright © 2016 by Marjorie Rosenberg

Edited by Dorothy E. Zemach.
Book design by DJ Rogers.
Published in the United States by Wayzgoose Press.

ISBN-10: 1-938757-23-8
ISBN-13: 978-1-938757-23-5

Table of Contents

Who This Book Is For

Many teachers create their own activities, either as a basis for a course or as supplementary materials to use along with a course book or other materials they are given. This short 'how to' book helps you discover different ways to present and write materials. There are awareness-raising tasks, a learning preferences questionnaire, tips for learners, information on learner strategies, and a comprehensive section with examples of activities including rubrics (written and oral instructions) and goals.

I hope this is an interesting, eye-opening and enjoyable manual to work through. My experience with different learner types has been all of the above.

It is necessary to mention, however, that there has been quite a bit of discussion recently as to the validity of learner types and learning preferences, and arguments both for and against can be readily found.

One of the problems mentioned is the large number of theories mentioned in the literature. Coffield (Coffield et al. 2004a, 2004b) set out to determine if any of these theories could be used by educators, and suggests that classifying people into a fixed set of characteristics may be counter-productive to learning.

Terminology has also been confusing as some of the same terms crop up and refer to different models, leaving teachers, trainers and writers in doubt as to which ones to use. Coffield and his colleagues in *Should We Be Using Learning Styles? What Research Has to Say to Practice* (Coffield et al. 2004a, 2004b) recommends six of the models they researched. Jill Hadfield, in an analysis of Coffield's work, recommends a total of seven, three of which are relevant to this module. In the article *Teacher Education and*

Trainee Learning Style (2006), Hadfield discusses whether learner types are determined from birth and unchangeable, or if learners have the option to move between different styles of learning. She goes on to say, "This is a crucial distinction, since many implications for classroom practice hang on the question of whether we consider learning styles to be fixed or mutable; namely how far we should match teaching techniques and tasks to learning styles and how far we should individualize instruction for different types of learner" (Jill Hadfield, *Teacher Education and Trainee Learning Style*, RELC Vol. 37, 2006, London).

We can say that 'learner types' and 'learning preferences' are basically the same. Learner types are generally thought of as characteristics we are born with, while preferences usually refer more to the behavior we exhibit while learning. These preferences grow out of our learner type and are used to help us learn, either consciously by choice or subconsciously because they make us more comfortable with what we are doing.

Two specific models recommended by Hadfield are the cognitive and behavioral ones, the first of which is addressed here. She goes on to mention modalities, also known as the visual, auditory, and kinesthetic model (VAK), and notes that the research done by Coffield et al. seems to concentrate on the idea of matching teaching style to individual learner types rather than on the concept of mixing teaching styles in order to reach a large number of learners. As Hadfield is in favor of an inclusive approach, she includes VAK in her list of learner types she considers to be important.

In looking at the arguments for and against, it seems to me that helping learners to stretch out of learner types when necessary, and teaching them strategies to do so, is a vital part of both materials development and classroom practice. Teaching strategies as well as thinking skills to learners can be incorporated into tasks written for the classroom. Hadfield points out that teachers need to have access to all learner types and learning preferences so they can pick and choose the particular ones that will be helpful for their learners. It is my contention that this applies as well to materials writers and developers. Most educators and writers tend to teach or write tasks in the way they themselves learn best, indicating that a varied and mixed approach is a positive way forward to help learners become successful and enjoy the process of learning a new language.

Aims

The basic aims of this book are to:

a) provide an overview of the basic categories of learner types (sensory-based perception: visual, auditory, kinesthetic emotional and kinesthetic motoric; and cognitive processing: global and analytic);

b) give examples of activities designed to appeal to particular learner types;

c) offer ideas on how to create activities to appeal to different learners;

d) look at ways to alter, adapt, and expand activities to make them appeal to different learner types and to help learners stretch out of their comfort zones.

1 Getting Started

Before you begin this book, read these short descriptions and do the tasks that follow.

Task 1A Processing Information

In order to store and recall information:

- **Visual** learners like to see words or images.
- **Auditory** learners like to hear words or sentences.
- **Kinesthetic emotional** learners like to involve their feelings and emotions.
- **Kinesthetic motoric** learners like to do something or touch something.
- **Global** learners like to have an overview.
- **Analytic** learners like to have details.

Think of examples of students from your classes who exhibit one of the above learning styles clearly.

Look at activities you have used and find a task that you feel would appeal more to one of the learner types mentioned than to the others. If you found any of these activities as downloadable resources online, file them so you can come back to them later.

Task 1B Matching Tasks to Learner Types

Look at these activities and decide which learners they would appeal to, based on the information on page 7. Remember that activities can appeal to more than one learner type.

a) Completing a text by listening to a recording
b) Having a discussion about a text
c) Completing a chart with figures
d) Matching sentence halves together
e) Finding names for objects in pictures
f) Exchanging personal information with a partner
g) Miming activities
h) Matching cards together
i) Finding or discussing the gist of a text
j) Describing words to a partner
k) Working in cooperative groups
l) Completing stem sentences

Read the Commentary for this task on page 70.

2 What Are Learner Types/Learning Preferences?

In the first task, I gave a very brief explanation of six different learner types. Here we are going to look more carefully at the definitions of learner types and their learning preferences.

Any observation of a class will lead to the conclusion that individuals take in and make sense of information in different ways. Although the ultimate goal of the teacher is to help learners reach a common level, the ways in which this is done can vary widely.

Research in the field has been carried out on sensory-based perception (what we see, hear, feel or touch) and on cognitive processing (how we organize the knowledge we both receive and possess into complete pictures or details, whether we prefer a complete picture or the details). Most researchers would agree, however, that learning preferences mean we use *filters* to make sense of the flood of information around us. These preferences then show up as particular characteristics, which are often recognized when learners interact with their learning environments.

We, and our learners, can become aware of habits and strategies that learners use to reach their goals. This is important to keep in mind when creating materials, as learners will react differently to both the presentation and the practice of language. Learners have different ways of becoming aware of new language features, and they process them and remember them differently. Keeping in mind that our learners are individuals is one of the tasks an ELT writer faces, and motivates us to look for a variety of ways to design materials.

Before you continue, use the questionnaire to determine your own learner profile. The explanations and information about the styles can be found in the commentaries that directly follow each questionnaire.

Task 2A Sensory-based Perception

Are you visual, auditory, kinesthetic motoric, or kinesthetic emotional?
Choose the sentences that are usually or generally true for you.

1. I remember words I have heard in songs or raps.
2. I remember where I last saw something.
3. I remember discussions we have in class.
4. I like to walk around while studying.
5. I enjoy working in groups with people I like.
6. I need to write words down to make sure I have spelled them correctly.
7. I remember best when the topic had a personal significance for me.
8. I repeat what I have learned out loud.
9. I learn well by doing role plays and miming.
10. I use highlighters or different colored pens when taking notes.
11. I feel best in a classroom that has a friendly and supportive atmosphere.
12. I generally have to try things out for myself in order to remember them.

Read the Commentary for this task on page 72.

Task 2B Cognitive Processing

Are you a global learner who processes information more holistically, or an analytic learner who processes it in a detailed and structured way? Choose the statements that are usually or generally true for you.

1. I need an overview before I start to learn.
2. I often work on more than one project at a time.
3. I remember the details better than the whole picture.
4. I relate what I am learning to my own life and experiences.
5. I prefer to learn in a structured, step-by-step way.
6. I like to work alone to avoid being distracted.
7. I like to get exact instructions from a teacher about to how to complete a task.
8. I sometimes overlook details.

Read the Commentary for this task on page 73.

3 Some Common Misconceptions about Learner Types and Learning Preferences

There are many opinions about learner types and their learning preferences. Look at the statements below and decide if they are true or false. Then check the task commentary explanations and answers.

Task 3 True or False?

1. Our learning preferences are fixed; they cannot be changed or adapted.
2. We learn best when we are taught in the way most comfortable for us.
3. Teachers can help to encourage learners to stretch out of their comfort zones.
4. Some learner types are better than others when it comes to learning.
5. Learning preferences are closely related to competence.
6. Each type has its strengths and weaknesses.
7. Trying out different methods can help learners to understand what they need.
8. Learner types give the teacher the opportunity to categorize learners.
9. Learner types are limiting.
10. Learning preferences provide learners with an excuse if they cannot learn something.

Read the Commentary for this task on page 74.

4 Learning Strategies of Different Learner Types

Learners tend to develop specific strategies either because they are comfortable or because they have had success with them in the past. However, most learners also learn to accommodate the type of teaching they experience. The following characteristics are general guidelines about individual style preferences.

Visual learners like to see words or illustrations and tend to write everything down. They often highlight or underline important words or phrases or make notes in the margin. They react well to visual stimulation such as images, drawings, and graphics. They often remember where they have seen something on a page, so they might need to relearn information in a different order than they first saw it so that they can easily remember it when they need to. This often means 'taking it off the page' – that is, putting it in a random order and learning it again.

Auditory learners like to listen or speak in order to remember. They may sub-vocalize while reading or move in rhythm. They love class discussions and often remember best what was discussed rather than what they read. They often learn sequentially and might need to re-learn material in a different order from what they first heard. Since they often repeat information aloud, it is good for them to write it down and learn it again in a different order to solidify it in their memory.

Kinesthetic emotional learners want to feel comfortable in a group. They like to connect learning with positive and personal experiences. These learners welcome the chance to be creative. They might have to learn to separate their feelings from what they need to learn.

Kinesthetic motoric learners like to try everything out for themselves. They learn by doing and through realistic situations. They like to move about or to work with cards and other things they can touch. They might need more frequent breaks than other learners. These learners need to learn to write things down that they have learned by moving about and reading them or saying the information aloud.

Global learners perceive information in a holistic manner and might want a complete overview before they start. They generally remember the entire experience better than the details. They usually enjoy working in groups and like establishing relationships with others. They should be given the chance to make use of their intuition, perception, and creativity. However, they might also need to separate learning from their feelings and may need to become more focused on the details at times.

Analytic learners like to get detailed and structured information. They often work best alone, as group work can be distracting. They are generally task-oriented and work purposefully to finish a job. They also enjoy working with facts more than with feelings. They appreciate logical explanations and specific goals. They might need to be reminded of the big picture so they do not get lost in the small details of a task.

5 Creating Activities for Visual Learners

Visual learners like colors, photos, pictures, images, charts, mind-maps, and so on. Activities that work well for them include labeling activities, describing pictures in writing, matching words to pictures, making predictions based on images, mazes, word searches, completing or creating mind-maps, filling in charts, and using maps. Several tasks for visual learners are described in detail below.

Giving Instructions to Visual Learners

Visual learners respond best to words that tell them to look at something or observe something. When you write or give oral instructions for visual learners, give information such as:

- Look at the picture and find four items you use every day.
- Write down three things that you see in this picture that begin with the letter '…'
- Picture a house and compare your ideas to the drawing on the page.
- Look at the drawing and label it with the words on the page.
- Use a red pen to circle the nouns and a blue pen to underline the verbs.

Labeling activities

Goal: Learners associate a vocabulary word with an image to help them remember it.

Begin with a picture or image that includes the vocabulary that needs to be taught. The picture or image should be large enough so that the learner can clearly find the information he or she is looking for. If the activity is to teach vocabulary, this can be in a box on the page or scattered around the image.

Here are several ways to create labeling activities:
1. Draw boxes or lines within the image for the learner to write the words in.
2. Have learners draw lines from a list of words to the part of the image they describe.
3. Number a list of words and have learners write the numbers into small boxes in the image.

Note: Images can be found through Creative Commons licensed websites and sites such as www.eltpics.com free of charge. There are also numerous sites that charge only a few dollars for images, both drawings and photos – search online for "stock photo site." You can also draw your own images, or ask some of your visual learners to help!

Activities using charts

Goal: Learners should be able to be able to remember the correct vocabulary based on the images they see on the charts. They also need to make use of their visualization skills by creating a chart based on a text.

1. Hand out / show with small pictures showing upward movement, downward movement, no movement, reaching a peak, and bottoming out. Include the necessary words describing to describe them. These can be drawn on the board, projected on a screen or be copied onto cards which are cut up and distributed to the class. (See Figure 1.)

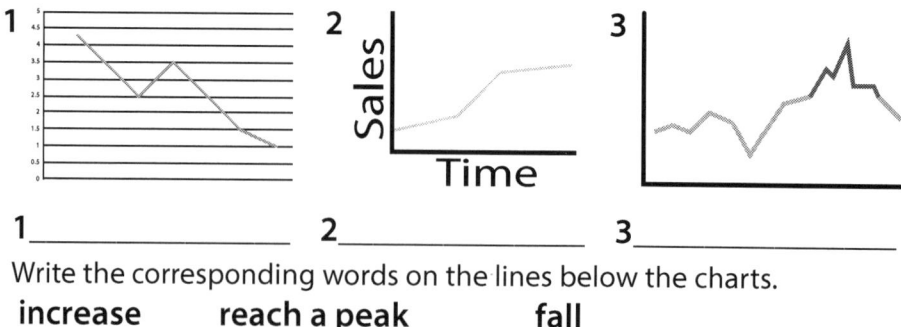

Write the corresponding words on the lines below the charts.

increase   reach a peak   fall

Figure 1: Charts and words

2. Once the learners are comfortable with the vocabulary, provide several charts showing movement and a separate set of sentences describing them. Learners then match them together. Examples:

A. Sales began by rising steeply, leveled off, and then dropped slowly over several months.

B. Profits fell sharply, bottomed out in the middle of the year, and then began to rise slowly.

3. For the third part of the exercise, give the learners a text describing a chart and a blank chart to complete after reading the text. (See Figure 2.) You can make charts in Word by clicking on 'Insert' and then 'Chart.'

Figure 2a: Blank graph

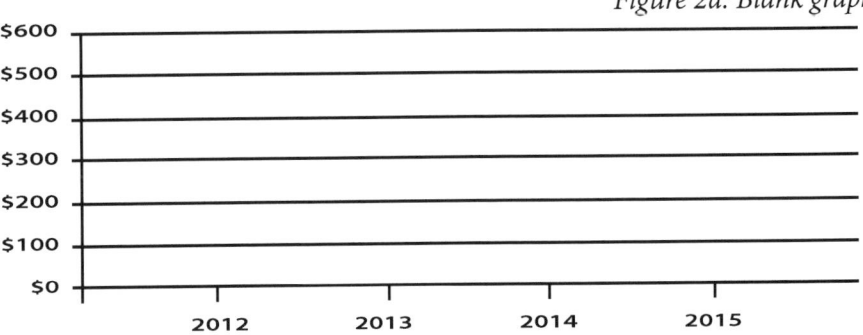

At the beginning of 2012, food cost a bit over $400 a month and fell to $250 in 2013. It then rose steadily till in 2015 it reached the same level it had been in 2012.

Figure 2b: Graph with lines drawn in

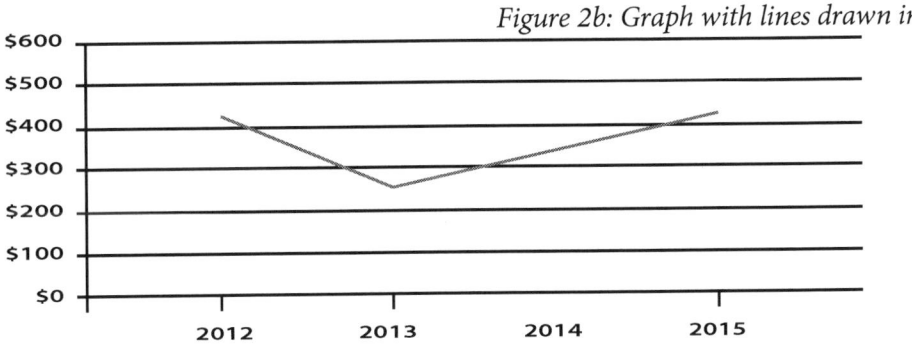

At the beginning of 2012, food cost a bit over $400 a month and fell to $250 in 2013. It then rose steadily till in 2015 it reached the same level it had been in 2012.

Crossword puzzles

Goals: These can be used to help learners to review vocabulary that they have come across or introduce new vocabulary
1. Create a standard one in which the learners have a blank puzzle and the clues. Learners fill in the puzzle using the clues.
2. Use small pictures instead of definitions as the prompts. Learners then fill in the words into the crossword puzzle.

There are several programs online that create crossword puzzles using words and definitions you supply. Limit the number of words depending on the level of the learners, but even with advanced groups, stay under twenty words. One program can be found at http://www.discoveryeducation.com/free-puzzlemaker/. Using this program, you can easily create and copy a crossword with definitions or text-based clues. If you want to use images, you need to find them yourself and add them manually (for example, by printing out the puzzle grid and then gluing or taping images beneath the grid).

Mazes

Goal: Learners practice or review collocations or grammar points and can check their own work.

Mazes can be used to practice collocations or grammar points. Begin with a box containing text (e.g. *I like …*) and two possible answers, labeled with different letters (e.g. a) *going to the movie theater*; b) *go to the movie theater*), only one of which is correct, Draw arrows from the first box to two other boxes, which also have similar sentences and arrows pointing to two more boxes. The learners continue to choose the correct answers, making note of the letters they have chosen, until they come to end of the maze. They then unscramble the letters to find the word describing the task. (See Figure 3.)

Read the sentences in the boxes. Choose the one that is grammatically correct and then move on to the next box. Use the letters you have chosen to fill in the missing word in the sentence below.

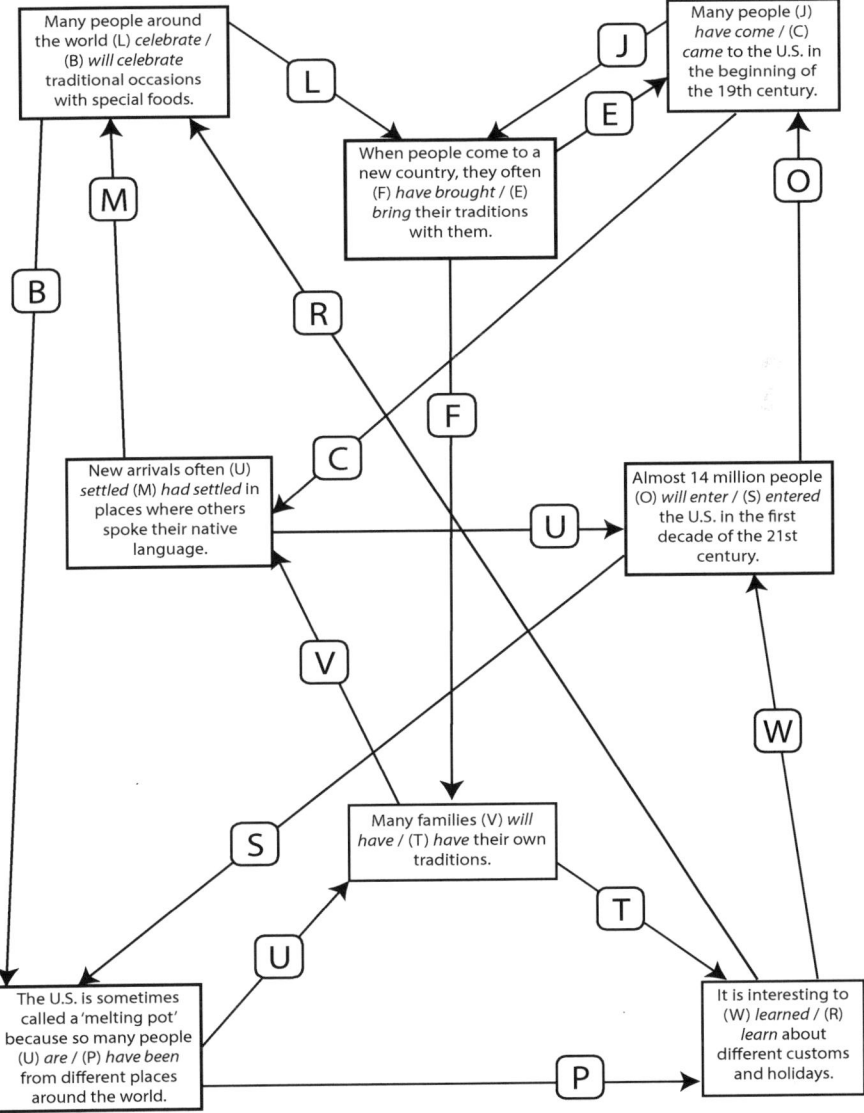

People from different _____ usually have their own traditions.

Figure 3: Maze

Visual word grid

Goal: Learners remember what words look like as the letters are put into boxes according to how they are written (e.g., 'a' is 'normal,' 'b' is a 'high' letter, and 'g' is a letter that goes below the line).

First, decide which vocabulary needs to be practiced, and put it into categories based on specific topics or parts of speech. Then create boxes that show the shapes of the letters of the words. (See Figure 4.)

Fruits	Vegetables	Grains	Dairy products
▢▢▢▢▢▢	▢▢▢▢▢▢▢	▢▢▢▢▢▢▢	▢▢▢▢▢▢
▢▢▢▢▢▢▢▢▢	▢▢▢▢▢▢▢	▢▢▢▢▢▢	▢▢▢▢▢▢▢▢▢
▢▢▢▢▢▢▢▢▢▢	▢▢▢▢▢▢	▢▢▢	▢▢▢▢▢▢
▢▢▢▢▢	▢▢▢▢▢▢▢▢▢	▢▢▢▢	▢▢▢▢▢▢

Put the words in the box into the correct categories.

| cream   carrot   cheese   cucumber   barley   kiwi |
| lettuce   apple   rice   nectarine   wheat   yoghurt |
| potato   cantaloupe   butter   rye |

Key:

Fruits	Vegetables	Grains	Dairy products
apple	carrot	barley	cheese
nectarine	lettuce	wheat	yoghurt
cantaloupe	potato	rye	butter
kiwi	cucumber	rice	cream

Figure 4: Visual word grid

Expanding on Activities

When expanding on activities, think about ways to help the visual learners. For example, visual learners tend to remember where they have seen something on the page, so making flashcards with vocabulary or sentences that they can review in a new order can help them to recycle and learn the necessary words or grammar.

6 Creating Activities for Auditory Learners

Auditory learners need to hear material and to talk about it with others. They like audio input and discussions in which they can take an active part. They enjoy activities in which they can describe words to each other, such as word grids and half crossword puzzles; activities in which they can orally describe something; and role plays, interviews, debates, oral drills, and speaking games such as 'Twenty Questions' or 'Who am I?' Several activities taking these points into account are described below.

Giving Instructions to Auditory Learners

Auditory learners respond best to instructions that tell them to listen to something, such as information, or to talk about something with another person. Write or give oral instructions to auditory learners such as these:

- Listen to the text and write down four items you own.
- Talk about this picture with your neighbor. Name five items beginning with the letter ' … '
- Listen to the speaker describe a scene. Then talk to your neighbor about what you heard.
- Listen for all the words referring to the environment in the audio recording.
- Ask your partner to tell you about his or her favorite activity.

Listening Comprehension Activities

Goal: Learners concentrate on words in a discussion and again while listening to a text.

Begin with a lead-in to a listening task that involves a guided discussion, either in pairs or groups or in open class. The discussion can include some of the words that will come later in the audio text or deal with the topic in such a way that learners can begin to expand on it themselves.

There are different ways to write listening comprehension tasks and these can be divided into before, during, and after activities:

Before:
- Tell learners the topic and have them make predictions about what they will hear. Then have them listen specifically to check their predictions. This can be as free predictions (e.g. *You are going to hear someone talking about shopping. What words do you think they will use?*) or sentences they check, such as: *You are going to hear someone check into a hotel. Check (√) the sentences you think you will hear. a) My name is ...,* b) *Is the room on the top floor?, c) Where is the elevator?*
- Tell learners the topic of an audio text, and have them predict with a group what vocabulary they think will hear. Then they listen to hear if their words were used, and if so, in which context.

During:
- Have learners make notes on specific lexis or grammar points while listening to a recording.
- Tell learners to fill in a chart or mind-map while listening.
- Ask learners to match a recording to a particular text or picture.
- Have learners complete a text while listening to a recording.

After:
- Check comprehension with true/false statements, gap fills, multiple choice statements, or open questions.
- Write a guided discussion dealing with points mentioned in the audio.
- Ask learners for an oral summary of the recording.
- Have learners write a summary of what they heard or their opinions about topics in the recording.

Note: Because auditory learners remember things sequentially (in the order they hear them), listening comprehension questions should follow the order of the recording.

When writing audio tasks for publishers, remember to specify as much as possible which accents the speakers should have as well as their ages, genders, and whether speech needs to be slowed down or can occur at a natural pace.

Discussion activities

Goal: Learners should remember a topic, lexis, or grammar point by having discussed it with others.

Write questions that learners can answer in pairs or groups. Make sure the questions are open ones, so learners are encouraged to speak and provide their own input. There are several possibilities for discussion activities in which learners:

- express opinions of an image or topic they have heard
- brainstorm uses for particular items in an image or audio text
- interview their partner about a topic and then report back to the class what their partner said

Word grids or half-crossword puzzles

Goal: Because auditory learners like to repeat things aloud in order to remember them, these activities help them more easily recall new lexis and use the vocabulary actively.

You can create word grids by using a table program in a word processing program. Choose the vocabulary words to be practiced and give each learner a grid that is half filled in. For example, Person A's grid has 5-7 words to explain and Person B's grid has the other 5-7 words. The rest of the grid for each student is empty, but the length of the word is indicated but the number of empty boxes.

Student A
Look at the words below and write down their definitions.
Read your definitions to Student B, who writes them into his/her grid. Listen to Student B's explanations and write the words into your grid.

1	F	R	A	C	T	I	O	N	S		
2	A	N	G	L	E	S					
3	P	E	R	I	M	E	T	E	R		
4	R	E	C	T	A	N	G	L	E		
5	P	L	A	C	E		V	A	L	U	E
6	R	A	D	I	U	S					
7											
8											
9											
10											
11											
12											

Math words

Student B
Look at the words below and write down their definitions.
Read your definitions to Student A, who writes them into his/her grid. Listen to Student A's explanations and write the words into your grid.

1											
2											
3											
4											
5											
6											
7	D	I	V	I	S	I	O	N			
8	E	Q	U	A	T	I	O	N			
9	T	R	I	A	N	G	L	E	S		
10	D	E	C	I	M	A	L	S			
11	D	I	A	M	E	T	E	R			
12	T	R	A	P	E	Z	O	I	D		

Figure 5: Word grid

Boxes that are not needed for the word can be filled in with black or gray, leaving the empty ones for the letters.

Give the learners time in pairs or small groups to come up with their own definitions for the words. Then put them in pairs and have them explain their words to each other.

The same type of activity can be done by giving learners a half-crossword. These can be produced using this link http://www.discoveryeducation. com/free-puzzlemaker/. While creating the puzzle, type the target word twice, separated by a space, and leave out the definitions completely. You will then have a blank puzzle that you copy twice – fill in half the words on the first puzzle sheet and the other half on the second.

Speaking Games

Who am I?

Goal: Learners gather information by asking questions and listening to answers.

Learners work in pairs, small groups, or whole class. Learners think of a famous person from history, their country, or a particular group (actors, sportspeople, scientists, etc.) They must know enough information about the person to answer questions One learner is chosen to begin, and the others ask questions that can be answered *Yes, No,* or *Maybe*. If someone asks a question that the learner cannot answer, that person can ask another question. The partner, group, or class tries to guess who the person is. This can be limited to twenty questions for efficiency. The same type of activity can be done as *Guess my job* or *Guess my country*.

Guess my word

Goal: Learners find words they need to practice and create their own explanations as well as listen to others' explanations of the vocabulary.

Have learners look at a text or a unit and choose five words they find difficult to remember. They then make sentences either describing the words or with a gap (they can say *dot, dot, dot* to make their partner say the word). This can be done with a time limit. At the end, partners tell each other which words they missed. If any mistakes were made, pairs work together to find a better way to describe the word or a better gap sentence for it.

What's the activity?

Goal: Learners practice making questions and remembering information they hear.

Learners choose an everyday activity. They can be given some example questions, such as *How often do you do it?, Where do you do it?, Do you do it alone?*, and *Do you need your hands/feet/head to do it?* Brainstorm other questions with the class. Put learners in small groups to ask each other the questions in order to guess the activity. Remind learners not to make their answers too easy or give away too much information.

Expanding on Activities

Remember that auditory learners respond best to language that asks them to listen or speak. Any expansion of an activity can instruct learners to discuss an issue, speak about something, listen for a word or topic, tell a partner how to do something, mention sentences or words they found interesting, discuss questions, tell a story, or summarize what they have heard. As they tend to remember the order in which they heard things, remind them to review material in a different order than they first learned it, so that they do not only remember the order of the information but the information itself. It is also helpful for auditory learners to write down what they have learned aloud.

7 Creating Activities for Kinesthetic Emotional Learners

Kinesthetic emotional learners like to get involved in what they are learning and find personal connections to material. They perform best when they can create positive feelings about learning in general. Activities that work well include:

- spontaneous role plays that they can personally relate to
- writing based on written or oral personalized input, and emotional images
- writing or speaking about personal experiences and opinions
- cooperative learning activities
- discussions about personal likes and dislikes
- expressing their opinions, wishes, and desires
- filling in questionnaires about themselves

Although they generally prefer group work, they need to feel safe in groups, and some learners may prefer to share very personal thoughts in writing meant for the teacher's eyes only.

Giving Instructions to Kinesthetic Emotional Learners

Kinesthetic emotional learners respond best to words telling them to feel or experience something. When you write or give instructions for kinesthetic emotional learners, give information such as:

- Look at the picture and write down three emotions you experience while looking at it.
- Talk with your partner and express how you feel about this topic.
- In pairs, describe your favorite place. Explain what it is that you especially like about it and why it is the place you most like to be.
- Imagine yourself in this scene and tell your partner what you are feeling.
- Write a short text on what you enjoy about learning and why.

Personalized Activities

Goal: Learners remember vocabulary or grammar because it is associated with something personal rather than abstract ideas.

Begin with a topic or image making use of the vocabulary or grammar point to be taught. There are several possibilities to personalize this material.

- Provide guided questions that require the learners to offer information about their likes, dislikes, wishes, plans, dreams, etc.
- Have learners interview each other in order to find out something about their partners related to the topic at hand.
- Have learners express their likes or dislikes for the topic and explain why they feel that way.
- Ask learners to discuss with a partner why they are learning English and their personal goals.

Cooperative Learning Activities

Goal: Learners find they can depend on teammates and experience positive feelings about learning to help them recall material.

Cooperative learning activities create groups that become interdependent on each other. Each person in the group has a particular task to fulfill, so everyone must work together to reach a goal. Some such activities are:

Home/Expert Groups

- Write three or four different texts with accompanying comprehension questions. Learners work in a small group and read only one of the texts and write out the answers to the questions together. These are the so-called *expert groups*.
- Learners then form new groups, the so-called *home group*s, that have at least one expert from each of the original groups.
- Each member in the group tells the others about the text they read and the questions they answered.
- Wrap up the activity by having each group give a summary of one

of the texts or by asking questions that someone in the group has to answer. Make it clear in the instructions that only those who were NOT experts are allowed to answer; but they are allowed to ask their experts before doing so. The teaching notes can include the questions to be asked.

Write the grid on the board and put the students' names into the boxes so that everyone knows who belongs where.

	Home Group A	Home Group B	Home Group C	Home Group D
Expert Group 1	Person A-1	Person B-1	Person C-1	Person D-1
Expert Group 2	Person A-2	Person B-2	Person C-2	Person D-2
Expert Group 3	Person A-3	Person B-3	Person C-3	Person D-3
Expert Group 4	Person A-4	Person B-4	Person C-4	Person D-4

Figure 6: Chart of home & expert groups

Cooperative crossword puzzles

Goal: Learners build confidence and work in a team to discover new vocabulary.

Go to http://discoveryeducation.com/free-puzzlemaker to create a crossword puzzle. Then write out four sets of clues for Learners A, B, C, and D. These clues must be used together to solve the puzzle. As an example, consider clues for the word *sugar*. Person A has the clue *This word is a noun*, Person B has *People use this in baking*, Person C has *This word begins with the letter 's'*, and Person D has *The plant this comes from grows in warm climates*. Depending on the level and the particular lexis, the clues can be partial definitions or give away more information to make it easier. Learners are then instructed to read each of the clues before guessing the word. They work together to solve the puzzle.

Surveys and questionnaires

Goal: Learners are helped to remember necessary information by personalizing it.

These can be used as a lead-in to a topic or as a review of a unit. Questions should be about the learners' opinions, feelings, or wishes – but not too personal, as these learners are generally quite sensitive and may not want to reveal their innermost feelings to others. Examples of safe questions include:

- What is your favorite food now and what was it when you were a child?
- How do you relax best?
- What kind of music do you like to listen to?
- Which characteristics do you look for in a friend?

The same type of activity can be used for discussions.

Writing based on personalized input

Goal: Learners work on cohesion and structure while expressing themselves.

Have learners first work on a grammar point, such as the use of the past tense. Then given them questions such as, *When was the first time you went to the movies alone?* or *When was the first time you cooked dinner for friends?* After practicing the form, give a writing assignment to write about an "important first" in their lives. Suggest topics or let learners choose their own.

Expanding on Activities

When expanding on activities it is helpful to use emotional language or language that encourages positive feelings and encouragement. Therefore, you can:

- Instruct them to discuss something enjoyable
- Ask them to write about favorite activities or places
- Encourage them to express personal views
- Talk or write about what they do well
- Provide them with emotional language to use in writing or speaking

Because they might need to learn to separate emotions from what they need to do, also give them tasks in which they simply have to describe something or write about it *without* mentioning their own feelings or opinions. This is essential in learning to write certain types of academic tasks or business letters, reports, and so on.

8 Creating Activities for Kinesthetic Motoric Learners

Kinesthetic motoric learners like to combine some type of movement with learning. They like to try things out on their own, and enjoy manipulatives (things they can touch or move around such as cards and dice or Cuisenaire rods), realia, and games. Because kinesthetic motoric learners prefer things to be concrete, they feel comfortable with lexis or boxed instructions (i.e., instructions set off from the rest of the text in boxes). Several different ideas are found below.

Activities include:
- Role plays in which they mime something
- *Find someone who…* games
- Running dictations
- Drawing lines to connect things in a book
- Dialogues they can act out
- *Describe and draw/do* games, in which a learner describes a picture to others who cannot see but are instructed to draw it, or describe something that others have to act out or do without seeing the words or illustration.
- Class games such as *bingo* and *tic tac toe*.

Giving Instructions to Kinesthetic Motoric Learners

Kinesthetic motoric learners respond best to words telling them to touch, move, or physically feel or experience something. When you write or give oral instructions such as:
- Find three items on the page that have moving parts.
- Complete the text below by drawing arrows to the missing sentences.
- Look at the picture and write down four of your favorite activities.
- Scan the text to find information about computers.
- Fill in the names of the missing objects under the headings.
- Follow the lines connecting the words to create collocations.

- Imagine you are doing an activity, such as making coffee or taking a break, and draw an arrow to the time of the day you do it. Then work in a small group and choose one of the activities. Act it out and have the others call out the activity and say when they do it.

Activities with Movement

Goal: Learners associate a movement with material they are learning to help them remember it later.

Begin with a word, short text, or image making use of the target vocabulary or grammar point. Here are several possibilities to add movement to a concept being taught:
- Have each person choose a word and a special movement to go along with it. First have them say the word as they make the movement. Then have them repeat this without saying the word but making the movement, while the others call out the word. Finally, have learners mime a process step-by-step. Others guess what they are doing and name the steps.
- Create activities for pairs in which each has to turn to a different page in the book and act out a role.
- Have learners circle or underline particular words or phrases.
- Have learners describe something to their partner, who draws it or acts it out.

Find someone who...

Goal: Learners should associate vocabulary with the movement they were doing at the time or the place in the room where they spoke with another learner.

Activities in which learners move around the room to gather information from others can be very helpful for kinesthetic motoric learners. These activities can be written to practice particular grammar points or lexis. For example, if the goal of the lesson is to teach the use of gerund and infinitive, instructions could be things such as, *Find someone who enjoys drinking tea in the afternoon* or *Find someone who needs to get up before*

6 am every day. To practice lexis, for example about jobs, write instructions such as *Find someone who uses spreadsheet programs at work* or *Find someone who is responsible for making appointments for other people.*

Bingo

Goal: Learners associate vocabulary with moving a coin or marker to a place on a sheet of paper or board.

Bingo cards are easy to create in a table program. Make eight – ten different tables, each with up to six words and print out the worksheets for the learners. (See Figure 7.) The teachers then reads out the definitions to the learners. Students place a coin on the word that matches the definition, and when their card is filled, they call out *Bingo!* This can also be done by giving learners a blank table and having them choose digital times from a list and writing them in the fields. The teacher then calls them out in the analogue form. For example, learners see 8:47, 6:13, 9:32, etc. and the teacher says the times out loud: *Thirteen minutes before nine, thirteen minutes after six,* or *twenty-eight minutes before ten.* The same idea can be done with irregular forms of the past tense: learners choose a particular number of words from a list, write them into a blank card and the teacher calls out the base forms while the learners cross off the corresponding words.

Student A

hole punch	shredder	stapler
filing cabinet	scissors	calculator

Student B

scissors	fax machine	hole punch
flash drive	pen	calculator

Student C

paper clips	shredder	printer
pencil	filing cabinet	stapler

Figure 7: Office Supplies bingo cards

Grammar bingo

Goal: Learners practice grammar by answering and asking questions and moving about the room.

Create a (grid) table with at least five boxes across and five down. Write out questions in different tenses in the boxes, such as *What were you doing yesterday morning at 8 am?* or *When did you last go to the dentist?* (See Figure 8.) Learners write short answers in each of the boxes. If they do not have enough room for a whole sentence, they can make notes (e.g., *swimming* could be the answer to *What were you doing on Sunday at 3 pm?* They need to give complete sentences when answering, however: *I was swimming.*) When students have finished, they find other people who have the same answers by moving around the classroom, asking each other the questions and answering those from their classmates. When they find someone whose answer matches, they write the person's name in the box. They call out *Bingo!* when they have five names in a row, either vertically, horizontally, or diagonally.

Grammar Bingo

Write the answers to the questions. Then find someone with the same answer.
Try to get five answers in a row (across, down, or diagonal) from five different people.
Then you can say 'Bingo'!

What were you doing on Saturday at 8 pm?	What haven't you done since you were a child?	What do you do every morning?	What are you going to do at the winter break?	What do you hope will happen next year?
What did you do yesterday?	What do you do several times a month?	What are you going to do next summer?	What do you do on the weekends?	What book are you reading?
How many films have you seen this year?	What are you going to do after class?	What did you enjoy doing as a teenager?	What are you studying?	Which sport have you never done?
What event do you think will be important next year?	What are you going to do this weekend?	What do you dislike doing?	What do you do in the evenings?	When did you begin to learn English?
When are you going to finish your studies?	What were you doing this morning at 9 am?	How many times have you been abroad this year?	Name one other class that you are taking.	How do you usually get to the university?

Figure 8: Grammar bingo

Tic tac toe

Goal: Learners work on specific grammar points and connect them with movement.

Draw a simple tic tac toe grid on the board. Ask learners which nine grammar points they want to practice, and write them into the grid. Put the class into two teams. Invite someone from the team to come to the board and write a sentence that practices (corresponds to) the particular grammar point, and if they get it right, they can mark an X or an O. The team which gets three Xs or Os in a row is the winner. .

Using cards

Goal: Learners learn vocabulary or sentence structure by playing with cards.

Create cards that can be matched together, such as words to pictures, descriptions of actions to drawings, sentence halves, or L1 to L2.

Once the cards are created, there are a variety of activities which can done with them.
- Match pictures to words or words to pictures
- Create cards depicting actions, put learners in groups, then have them take turns and choose a picture card from a pile of cards turned upside down. Instruct the learner who drew to card to mime it and have the others guess what he /she is doing.
- Create cards with pictures or drawings on them. Give each learner five or six cards and instruct them to lay the cards in front of them. Then say the words which describe or match the words out loud. When a learner hears a word that matches a card, he or she turns the card over. When one of the learners has turned over all his or her cards, he/she calls out *Bingo!*

Running dictations

Goal: Learners move about the classroom and remember text they have read.

Hang up several copies of a text around the room. Put the learners in groups and have them choose one runner who runs to one of the texts, then comes back to the group and tells what he/she remembers of it. The others write it down. This continues until the text is finished. Alternatively the group can rotate runners and take turns. When the groups are finished, they compare the original with their version and make any necessary corrections. Dialogues or audio texts in a book can be adapted so that learners read an excerpt and have to run to the board to write it down.

Expanding on Activities

Remember that kinesthetic motoric learners respond best to language that includes movement or tactile words, so encourage learners to *do* something. This can include circling or underlining words, turning to a partner and doing something, explaining what they experienced when they did something, or miming activities. They often learn well while moving, so have them write down what they have just learned.

9 Creating Activities for Global Learners

Global learners like to see an overview or general concepts before getting into the details. They also tend to use their emotions more than their analytic thought processes. Activities that work well for them include

- unjumbling words, putting sentences or texts in the correct order
- activities to practice cohesion
- paraphrasing
- spontaneous role plays
- writing based on experiences
- filling in time lines
- making creative sentences from groups of words
- storytelling or predicting endings to stories.

Use a variety of these tasks to appeal to global learners. Remember that global learners need to find ways to organize their material and to create their own overviews if they are not given one. They also like to make use of creativity and their imagination. Ideas for activities are below.

Giving Instructions to Global Learners

Global learners respond best to words telling them to be aware of an entire concept or idea, as well as the more emotional side of learning. When you write or give oral instructions for global learners, give information such as:

- Look at the chart and name the general trends over the year.
- Create a mindmap explaining the experiences you had on your last holiday.
- Read the text and write four general ideas you found there. Then predict your own ending.
- Look at the sentences / paragraphs and talk to your partner about the topic of the text. Then put the sentences / paragraphs into the correct order.
- Choose one of the topics below and create a role play with your

partner. Act it out in front of the class.
- Look at the images on the page and decide what the general topic could be.

Activities that Use Ordering

Goal: Learners are helped to understand cohesion by putting sentences or paragraphs together.

Begin with a sentence or phrase that gives a general idea of the topic of the activity. For example, if you are talking about food, you could say that the topic for the day is fast food restaurants versus home-cooking; or if you are talking about lifestyle, it could be rural versus urban living. Have learners discuss the topic with a partner or the whole class and suggest vocabulary or ideas for the topic.

Next, give the learners a list of linking words or cards with linking words on them. Have them write a text and incorporate the linking words into it. Alternatively, give a list of rules about word order such as, "adjectives before nouns," "adverbs after verbs," etc., and have them write a text keeping these rules in mind.

Here are several ways to create ordering activities.
- Jumble sentences by writing them in an incorrect order and having learners put them together. You can separate the chunks of language with slashes, or even cut up strips of paper.
- Give parts of sentences and have learners add the missing elements.
- Scatter sentences or paragraphs on the page or put them in boxes in an incorrect order. Number them so that answers can be easily checked in class.
- When ordering sentences, write linking words on the page for learners to choose from to create a cohesive text.
- Have learners order paragraphs and slot them into a text; or put an entire text together.

Using storytelling

Goal: Learners should be able to be able to structure a text and make use of cohesive elements by putting a story together using prompts.

Begin with images of different symbols, drawings, or words. These can be based on fantasy, such as a unicorn or a symbol for money. You can find such symbols in Word or in free clip art programs. Add various linking words on the page. If linking words have not yet been taught, you could substitute a matching activity to clarify their meaning.

Put learners into small groups and have them come up with a theme that matches the symbols or picture they have. If the pictures represent fantasy items like unicorns, the overall theme could be fairy tales or medieval stories; if the pictures show features of modern life, the overall theme could be shopping or the environment, and so on. Themes are up the learners to decide. Learners then choose symbols or images that appeal to them and relate to the overall theme they chose, and use them to create a story. Give students time to work out the ideas and set up a structure.

The final task can be given as homework – if the class has a wiki, the group could continue to work together, or each student could write an individual story. Alternatively the group could produce the story in class and then write it out at home, so you could correct it. Learners could also leave the ending out and have others predict or create their own ending to the story.

Completing stem sentences

Goal: Learners see sentences as whole structures and complete unfinished ones.

These activities can be used to practice specific grammar or vocabulary. For example, to practice the gerund vs. infinitive, give learners the same group of stems and asked to finish them using their own words, opinions, situations, experience, etc. Learners then give you their sentences and you hand them out randomly to others in the class. Students then read them aloud and ask the whole class who they think wrote them. Some examples of stem sentences include:

- *I always enjoy…*
- *I have never been good at…*
- *Next year I want to…*
- *I am not looking forward to…*
- *I am now ready to…*
- *I really need to…*
- *Last year I gave up…*
- *When I was a child, I used to…*

Mind maps

Goal: Learners create and discuss information based on a global illustration which connects different elements.

Although mind maps also include details, the idea of connecting ideas and seeing them as a complete picture appeals to global learners. Making these mind maps personal and allowing learners to fill them in as they choose allows global learners to make use of their creativity. Maps can then be discussed with a partner, as global learners often enjoy working with others. They can also use them to organize material they are presented with. (See Figure 9 for a simple mind map.)

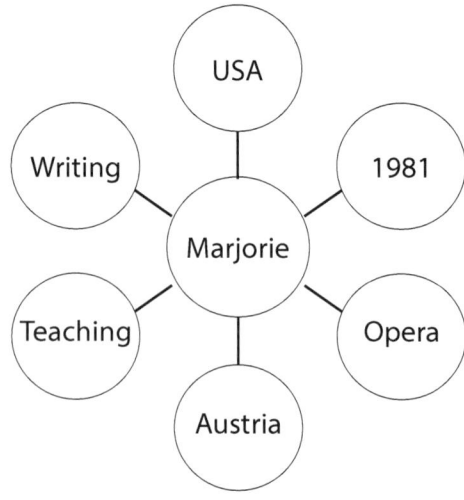

Figure 9: Mind map

Expanding on Activities

When expanding on activities, remember that global learners respond to fairly general language, as well as language that takes the humanistic side into account. When Because they may have problems when presented with too many details at one time, or feel uncomfortable when they have to use someone else's structure or analyze something based on a set of criteria, remind them to find a way to prioritize the tasks on a page and understand that structure in some cases is more important than spontaneity. Give them activities to follow up with that allow them to put their thoughts into a structure they create themselves.

10 Creating Activities for Analytic Learners

Analytic learners like to see structure and detail about a topic. They usually work on one thing at a time, and prefer to go step-by-step through an exercise or learning experience. They also like to know exactly what they are expected to do. Activities that work well include

- word grids
- matching activities
- logic puzzles
- various forms of multiple choice, error correction,
- and true/false statements
- writing based on facts
- guided discussions
- analyzing charts or figures
- working with word families

Use a variety of these tasks to appeal to analytic learners.

Giving Instructions to Analytic Learners

Analytic learners respond best to language pointing out facts, details, or logic. Because the end result is important for them, explain what the finished task will look like (e.g., a text-writing exercise can include the number of paragraphs expected as well as the number of words). When you write or give oral instructions for analytic learners, give information such as:

- Look at the chart and find the figures that indicate a large, small, or medium change.
- Place these inventions on the timeline using logic to decide which invention came first and is the most recent one.
- Look at the photo and analyze the situation. Discuss it with your partner and decide on a logical solution to the problem.
- Read the sentences and mark the subject, verb, object, etc.

- Decide which of the following sentences can be changed into passive voice and why. Then make the necessary changes.
- Read through the text and find the mistakes. Some lines are correct, others have one mistake in them. Check (√) the ones that are correct, and fix the ones that have a mistake.

Matching Activities

Goal: Learners use their analytical thought processes to decide which sentence halves or words and definitions belong together.

Begin by explaining that learners have to match sentence halves together or definitions to vocabulary. Have them first scan the exercise for any words they don't know and go over these first. Then let them work alone or in pairs to match the sentence halves or the definitions to the words.

There are several ways to write matching activities.
- Write out heads and tails of sentences to match together. The actual matching can be based on grammar, vocabulary, or linking words. (See Figure 10.)
- Create definitions of words and have learners match them to the words. To make it more challenging, you can give two extra definitions or sentence tails so that learners have to decide which ones not to use.

Sentence halves (with extra 'tails')

Match the sentences halves together. There are two endings you do not need.

1 I always enjoy	A to see the new movie on TV.
2 He never	B studying at home?
3 She wants	C eats breakfast at 7:30 am.
4 Does he usually	D work on holidays.
5 I think she	E going to the movie theater.
6 We don't like to	F meet friends on the weekend?
	G are fun to talk with.
	H is a really nice person.

Figure 10: Heads/tails matching

- Create a word grid and have learners fill in words based on definitions or gapped sentences. (See Figure 11.)

	Definitions									
1	A communication system using sounds, words, grammar, etc.								░	░
2	Units of language that have meaning					░	░	░	░	░
3	A way to explain what something is or means									
4	A single bit of information					░	░	░	░	░

Answer key:

	Definitions									
1	A communication system using sounds, words, grammar, etc.	l	a	n	g	u	a	g	e	░
2	Units of language that have meaning	w	o	r	d	s	░	░	░	░
3	A way to explain what something is or means	d	e	f	i	n	i	t	i	o	n
4	A single bit of information	d	e	t	a	i	l	░	░	░

Figure 11: Word grid

- Create a magic square as shown in the image and have learners fill in the words based on definitions. When they have done it correctly the squares will add up to 15 in all directions (across, down and diagonally). (See Figure 12.)

☐ town hall	☐ parking lot	☐ bank	=15
☐ public library	☐ city park	☐ bus stop	=15
☐ police station	☐ florist	☐ grocery store	=15
=15	=15	=15	

1. If you want to find a book to read or use a computer, you can go to the _____.

2. When you need to get money from your account, you can go to the _____.

3. If you need flowers for a special occasion, the _____ can help you.

4. If you need something for dinner, have a look at the _____.

5. The _____ is a good place to relax or to have a walk.

6. When you need something done officially, you may have to go to the _____.

7. If you drive to town, you may need to look for the _____.

8. If you lose something, you can ask for help at the _____.

9. If you use public transport, you can wait at the _____.

Key

6	7	2
1	5	9
8	3	4

Figure 12: Magic square

Timelines

Goal: Learners think about specific points of time in their own lives or those of others and ask questions about them.

Draw a timeline as a straight or a curved line on the page or have learners draw their own. Give learners a particular task such as their personal timelines for a given period in their lives and ask them to fill in dates or events. Have them discuss the finished timelines in pairs or groups. They can be encouraged to ask open questions, such as *What happened in 2005?* or *When were you in London?* Depending on the type of class, these timelines can also be based on a particular topic such as studies or points in someone's working life. They can then be collected (or copied, if necessary) and hung up about the room. Learners then walk around and try to guess which timeline belongs to whom. If this is given as homework, learners could also attach photos of themselves at relevant points in the timeline.

This example (Figure 13) mixes years and events.

Examples of questions:
What happened in 1975?
When did you move to Austria?
When did you first present at a conference?
When was your first conference presentation?

Figure 13: Timeline

Word families

Goal: Learners see the relationship between roots and other forms of words.

These are often presented with a root and other forms of the word. Analytic learners find it a good way to increase their vocabulary. Figure 14 shows a completed grid. Learners can be given part of the grid and asked to fill it out, or they can work in pairs, each with different words in the grid, which they have to explain to their partners. Gapped sentences can be added for more practice.

verb	noun	adjective	adverb
(to) direct	director	direct	directly
(to) agree	agreement	agreeable	agreeably
(to) believe	belief / believer	believable	believably
(to) create	creation / creator	creative	creatively
(to) imagine	imagination	imaginable	imaginably

Figure 14: Word family chart

Working with facts

Goal: Learners work with facts to understand texts.

Give learners a series of facts to slot into a text, or a text from which they need to pull out certain facts. This can be done in writing or orally. Another option is to present learners with a series of facts for them to judge as true, false, or possible, which they do by reading the text. More advanced groups can make up their own true, false, and possible statements after reading a text and quiz other groups.

Expanding on Activities

Because analytic learners often prefer to work on their own and set their own goals, expansion of activities should allow them to do one task at a time. It is also important to make clear to them exactly what is expected. Therefore, instructions should be detailed and give the information step-by-step. As they may get stuck in the details, these learners should be reminded that sometimes the finished product is more important than each part of the task; they may need to take a step back from the details to remember the big picture.

11 Activities Arranged According to Learner Type

Here are some handy lists to remind you of the types of activities that suit different learner types. In order to ensure a good mix in the classroom, you can aim to include a variety of activities in a typical lesson or throughout a course.

Visual

- Crossword puzzles
- Labeling activities (with and without the given words)
- Describing pictures by writing
- Matching pictures to words
- Predictions based on a picture
- Mazes
- Finding a word based on size of box as for letter
- Word searches (with and without definitions)
- Matching descriptions to pictures
- Filling in charts
- Filling in or creating mind-maps
- Listening comprehensions using images
- Searching for information in a text
- Using maps

Auditory

- Word grids and half-crossword puzzles (describing words to each other)
- Describing pictures by speaking
- Discussions following a text
- Discussions following audio input
- Guided discussions
- Guided role plays
- Writing based on oral input

- Speaking game: *Who am I?*
- Speaking game: *Say my word*
- Speaking game: *Guess my job*
- Spelling words to each other
- Speaking game: 20 Questions
- Listening comprehensions using images
- Guided interviews
- Debates based on texts
- Completing pictures by following oral instructions
- Guided discussions (with questions, with information, with goals to reach)
- Matching texts to audio
- Oral drills
- Brainstorming activities
- Jigsaw reading
- Story telling
- Debates
- Using songs
- Speaking in pairs or groups
- Taking notes or minutes in meetings
- Describing graphs to each other

Kinesthetic Emotional

- Spontaneous role plays
- Writing based on written personalized input
- Writing based on emotional oral input
- Writing based on emotional images
- Writing based on personal experiences or opinions
- Cooperative learning activities (helping each other in team work)
- Discussions on personal likes and dislikes
- Expressing opinions, wishes, desires
- Filling in personal questionnaires and surveys
- Jokes

Kinesthetic Motoric

- Speaking game: *What am I doing?*
- Speaking game: *Find someone who...*
- Speaking game: *Find out about...* (a person)
- Class games: Bingo / Tic Tac Toe
- Running dictations
- Responding by raising hand or standing when words are heard in text
- Drawing lines to connect words or sentences
- Acting out dialogues
- Describe and draw

Global

- Ordering a text
- Spontaneous role plays
- Slotting sentences in a text (understanding cohesion)
- Slotting paragraphs in a text (understanding cohesion)
- Putting paragraphs in the correct order (understanding cohesion)
- Completing stem sentences (using own ideas)
- Making creative sentences from groups of words
- Writing answers to open questions
- Unjumbling words
- Paraphrasing
- Writing fantasy texts based on written information or images
- Predicting the end of a story
- Story-telling

Analytic

- Word grids (filling them in based on definitions)
- Matching words to definitions
- Gap texts
- Logic puzzles
- Acrostic puzzles
- Filling in correct tenses
- Multiple choice possibilities:
- Multiple choice words in a text: *(I like a) watch; b) watching TV.)*
- Multiple choice words to test comprehension after reading or listening to a text: *(The man bought a) a newspaper; b) a magazine; c) a book.)*
- Multiple choice comprehension sentences after reading or listening to a text: *(The writer talked about a) the ecological problems in developing countries; b) climate change in developed countries; c) pollution around the world.)*
- Error correction (changing words, or correcting spelling and word order)
- Making questions based on the answers
- Changing sentences from one tense to another
- True/false questions
- Choosing the correct answer to a question
- Writing based on written input of facts
- Translating words
- Translating sentences
- Completing stem sentences (with prescribed information)
- Categorizing items
- Filling in a timeline (based on supplied information)
- Heads and tails (matching beginnings and endings of sentences together; can be based on grammar, structure, word order, or vocabulary)
- Guided discussions (with questions or vocabulary)
- Searching the Internet for specific information
- Working with word families (making nouns from verbs, making opposites, etc.)
- Analyzing charts and figures

- Adding punctuation to sentences
- Parallel writing
- Preparing mini-presentations that have to conform to certain constraints, such as time constraints or using particular vocabulary
- Magic square (for vocabulary)

Task 4

Look at the lists of activity types and choose one activity from each of the six categories. Think about what makes it appeal more to one learner type more than another. Then read the commentary here for general information about what makes tasks especially appeal to a particular learner type. You can also look back at the commentary for Task 1 for more information.

> Read the Commentary for this task on page 76.

Task 5

Now look at the activities you have chosen and find ways to make them appeal to another learner type.

> Read the Commentary for this task on page 77.

Task 6

Look at the grid of activity types and choose one activity from each of the six categories. Write a task using rubrics and goals that primarily appeal to a particular style. Add an extension of the task that helps learners stretch out of their style and appeals to other types as well. Try out the task with your learners and get feedback from them about what aspects of the task helped them to learn.

12 Giving Instructions

We use language to appeal to different learner types, primarily with the sensory-based learner types. When creating activities we need to give instructions, both written and verbal, for different types of learners. Therefore, being familiar with the language that learners are comfortable with is a valuable asset. First impressions often come through our senses, and learners may understand a task better if they are told to read, listen, move, or use their feelings to carry it out. As mentioned earlier, we tend to teach or write in the way we ourselves think; therefore, giving thought to a wide range of language in order to explain tasks will make instructions more learner-friendly.

Task 7 Part 1

Decide which of these words would most likely appeal to these different learner types. Some may be for more than one type.
agree, tell, describe, stress, look at, view, join, feel, listen, picture, ask, read, touch, see, act out, speak, dialogue, support, discuss, conversation, draw
> Visual
> Auditory
> Kinesthetic Emotional
> Kinesthetic Motoric

Task 7 Part 2

Look at the instructions below and identify the sensory-based language; i.e., language which is related to our senses of seeing, hearing, feeling (emotions), and touching. Then say which type of learner you think the instructions and the task would appeal to and why. Each task may appeal to more than one type of learner.
> 1. Look at the table below. It shows a useful way to learn and record vocabulary. Fill in the missing words.

2. Listen to the three conversations. Then tell your partner which topics were discussed.

3. Read these strategies to keep a conversation going. Do you agree with them? Why or why not?

4. You are going to read an article from which four sentences have been removed. Put them into the correct places by looking for cohesion markers.

5. Describe the picture you see to your partner, who draws it. Your partner can ask you questions but cannot see the picture you are describing.

6. Listen to the dialogue and decide if the following statements are true or false. Give reasons for your answers.

7. Work in a group. Act out an everyday activity for the others to guess.

Read the Commentary for this task on page 78.

13 Analyzing Activities

Task 8

Look at the activities and decide which type of learners these activities would appeal to most. Identify the elements that would suit these different learner types, taking into account the information about learner preferences in Chapter 4 and the specific information about activities in Chapters 5 – 10.

Example 1: Gap fill with cards

Put learners into small groups. Copy and cut up one set of cards per group. Copy the gap text for each of the learners. Have learners match the cards together and write the appropriate collocations into the gaps.

Note: This is a shortened example as the original had more words.

Collocations gapped sentences

Cards

account	➤	➤	number
break-even	➤	➤	point
profit	➤	➤	margin
mission	➤	➤	statement
cash	➤	➤	cow
bottom	➤	➤	line

Figure 15: Collocations gap fill

Gapped sentences

1. When a customer calls with a bookkeeping question, we have to ask for his or her _____.
2. Because of the money we have put into research and development since the start of the first quarter, our _____ is higher than it was last year.
3. Due to increased production costs, we have had to raise prices on several items to maintain a_____ on these products.
4. Companies often create a _____ to inform their stockholders and employees about their aims, values, purpose, and future direction.
5. We should thank our R&D department for this incredibly successful product, which has turned into a _____ for us and helped us through some difficult times.
6. At the departmental meeting, we don't need to go into all the details of the project. The decision-makers are only interested in hearing about the _____.

Example 2: The Language Auction

Make a list of phrases or grammar points your learners have had trouble with. Write the phrases in the grid, copy it, and hand out one copy to each learner. (See Figure 16.)

Put learners into small groups or pairs. Have them look at the sentences and make corrections. The group then discusses the corrections and agrees on how many points they are willing to bet on each of them. Go through the correct answers with them. For each correction that is right, the learners get the number of points they bet. If their answer is wrong, they lose the number of points they bet.

Sentence auction

Sentences	Points bet	Points won	Points lost
1. I am going to university every day.			
2. He wants that she phones him daily.			
3. I am going to see them today evening.			
4. Did she went to California last week?			
5. They sing more better then we do.			
6. I am here since 7 a. m.			
7. They have seen her yesterday.			
8. Me and Susan like to go to the movie theater.			
9. Always they eat breakfast.			
10. I enjoy see my friends on the weekend.			
TOTALS			

Figure 16: Language auction

Example 3: All About Me

Put students into pairs and give each of them a copy of the worksheet. Tell them to They then pretend that they are their partners, and complete the sentences according to how they think their partner would complete them. When they finish, they either exchange papers and read what the other person wrote and comment, or read their sentences aloud and discuss the answers with their partners. The task can be extended to homework by having students write a short story about their partners based on the information they got in the activity.

All About Me

When I was a child, I wanted to be a _____ when I grew up.

My favorite color is _____ because _____.

I have always been good at _____.

My favorite foods include _____.

When I have free time, I usually _____.

Something I am afraid of is _____.

Something most people do not know about me is _____.

Figure 17: All About Me worksheet

Read the Commentary for this task on page 80.

14 Creating Self-Study Material

Self-study material for learners can also be geared to different learner types. Looking back at the information in this book, do Task 9 and read the commentary.

Task 9 Part 1

Decide which of these types of activities for self-study would appeal to the different learner types. (Each appeals to more than one type of learner.)

a) Completing a gapped text with words from a box

b) Listening to a dialogue and answering multiple choice questions

c) Completing a mind-map with vocabulary terms

d) Doing a crossword puzzle

e) Listening to a text and choosing the correct summary (out of three different ones)

f) Finding hidden objects in a picture

g) Matching sentences halves together

h) Creating different collocations with a set of verbs and using them in sentences about themselves

i) Predicting what a newspaper headline might mean

j) Matching idioms to pictures

k) Matching dialogues to cartoon drawings

Read the Commentary for this task on page 81.

15 Reflection

This book has presented you with new ideas and concepts. Take some time to do the last task, and think about yourself, how you learn, your students, and what you can do to help them in the future.

Task 10

Answer these questions:

1. When you learn yourself, what do you do to help yourself remember and recall information?
2. Did you recognize any of your students in the descriptions? If so, what helped you to recognize them?
3. What new information did you learn from reading this book and doing the tasks?
4. If you have been writing tasks for learners, what will you now change about this process?

Glossary

Analytic learner: A learner who learns best by concentrating on details and analysis of problems

Audio-lingual method: A method used to teach foreign languages which concentrates on listening and speaking before reading and writing

Auditory learner: A learner who learns best by listening and speaking

Cognitive processing: The process of thinking

Cohesion: Creating text which is unified and flows easily from one part to another

Collocations: Pairs or groups of words which are habitually used with each other

Comfort zones: A state in which people feel comfortable and can operate without stress or anxiety

Coping strategies: Specific behavioral or psychological actions that people use to master or minimize situations that cause stress

Creative commons license: A license granted to someone who is willing to share work such as photographs or written materials

Global learner: A learner who learns best when using the whole picture

Global-analytic model: A learning style model that looks at two ends of a scale to determine style/preferences; one end is very detailed-based and the other is more holistic

Kinesthetic learner: A learner who learns best when using touch, movement or emotions

Modalities: How learners use their senses in the learning process. These are commonly broken down into visual (seeing), auditory (hearing), kinesthetic (moving) and tactile (touching).

Motoric: The movement used by some kinesthetic learners

Multi-tasking: Being able to do more than one thing at a time

NLP: Neuro-linguistic programming, a form of therapy developed in the 1970s in the US by Richard Bandler, John Grinder, and Robert Dilts, which has been used as well by educators for sensory-based instruction, classroom management, establishing rapport, and goal-setting, and so on.

Realia: Authentic materials used in the classroom

Rubric: The instructions to the learner preceding a task

Sensory-based perception: understanding the world around you through the use of the five senses

Stretching strategies: Methods to help learners move out of their most comfortable styles, used primarily when a learner preference is not the strategy best suited to a particular task

Suggestopedia: A teaching method developed by the Bulgarian psycho-therapist Georgi Lozanov in the 1970s in which various methods, including music and relaxation techniques, are used to help people learn foreign languages

Visual learner: A learner who learns best by seeing

Resources

Hadfield, Jill (2006). *Teacher Education and Trainee Learning Style*, in RELC Vol. 37(3), SAGE Publications, London, pgs. 369-388.

Hadfield, Jill (1992). *Classroom Dynamics*, Oxford University Press, Oxford, UK.

Rosenberg, Marjorie (2013). *Spotlight on Learning Styles*, Delta Publishing, Peaslake, UK.

From the Author

I have been fascinated by the different ways people learn since I was first introduced to the concept at a seminar on Suggestopedia in Salzburg in the 1980s. As someone who struggled with a foreign language in high school in the US, it was a relief to discover that the problem I had had was with the method rather than with my particular abilities to learn a second language. As we were taught using a strictly audio-lingual method, and actually 'forbidden' to make pictures of the words in our heads, discovering that I was a visual learner explained why this method had been such an abject failure for me.

This realization led to find out as much as I could about the ways in which people perceive, process, and recall information, and the effect this has on learner success. After attending seminars on learning styles and competing an NLP master practitioner and a trainers' course in the US, I attended a course given for teachers by Michael Grinder, the brother of John Grinder, one of the founders of NLP. Michael was the first person to begin using the NLP techniques, which dealt with perception, processing, storage, and recall, in a systematic way to help teachers in the classroom. This eye-opening course led me to find ways to help my own EFL students in the adult education courses I taught, and became the basis for the teacher training courses I held jointly in Austria with a colleague who was using many of the ideas to teach math. We designed our own visual, auditory, kinesthetic (VAK) questionnaires and continued observation of both learners and teachers, which eventually resulted in our splitting the kinesthetic learner into two separate types, the emotional and the motoric, which had traditionally been grouped together.

At more or less the same time, I became acquainted with April Bowie of the Learning Styles Institute in Seattle. Washington. Through April I learned about the original work done on modalities (VAK) by educators Walter Barbe and Raymond Swassing, as well as Rita and Kenneth Dunn and the global–analytic model first developed by Hermann Witkin. Witkin was a psychologist who noticed that fighter pilots in the US military during

World War Two reacted differently to low visibility conditions; some kept their planes upright and others actually began to fly upside-down. Witkin thereby concluded that there were two types of cognitive processing going on, the field-dependent (global) and the field-independent (analytic). He suggested that those more influenced by their environments (global learners) were more easily distracted, but also relied on an overview; while those less influenced by what was going on around them (analytic) could close out these distractions and concentrate on the facts. This began to become better known in the world of education, and the Group Embedded Figures Test is still used today to determine learner styles. April and I worked together for almost 10 years, although we lived some 6,000 miles apart. When she passed away in 2006, my mission became to continue with the work she had begun.

Over the years, I have incorporated learning styles and preferences into a variety of books, both for the classroom and supplementary teachers' resource material. The first one of these, published in 2001 by the Austrian National Publisher, was *Communicative Business Activities*, which included questionnaires for the VAK and global-analytic learning styles, with activities marked for the type of learner they were designed for. After that, I worked on a number of textbooks for Austrian schools in which we added learning preference profile checklists and learning tips for students, as well as teaching notes for teachers.

In 2013 Delta Publishing brought out my book *Spotlight on Learning Styles*, which includes information about learning preferences, learner and teacher characteristics and strategies, questionnaires to determine preferences, and activities written to both appeal to particular learner types as well as to help learners stretch out of their style. For me, knowing about preference has helped me to become much more tolerant of learners whose styles are different from my own, as well as to give learners tips when they ask for them. In a research project at the University of Graz, we discovered that learners rarely give thought to how they learn and are quite appreciative of the opportunity to do so. Some had even tried to change their normal habits in order to please parents or teachers and were actually relieved to find that what they were doing was normal for their individual profile.

1 Commentary: Task 1B Processing Information (p. 8)

a) This appeals mostly to auditory learners because the main task is understanding spoken language. There is some appeal to visual learners when they look at the text, and also to analytic learners as the answers may fall into logical categories of parts of speech or particular grammar usage.

b) This appeals mostly to auditory learners because they need to both speak and listen, and to analytic learners because it deals with hard facts.

c) This appeals mostly to visual learners, who like to see charts and other graphic organizers. It also appeals to analytic learners, who will generally search for a logical way to complete a chart.

d) This appeals mostly to analytic learners because they usually base their answers on logical sequences. It can also appeal to visual learners because it deals with written text. If done as pair or group work, it can also appeal to auditory learners as they discuss the possibilities.

e) This appeals mostly to visual learners, who enjoy seeing pictures. Done in groups, it could also be auditory, as the learners would presumably discuss their opinions.

f) This appeals mostly to kinesthetic emotional and global learners because both value feelings and emotions. They also like to find out about other people, and look for ways to set up relationships with others.

g) This appeals mostly to kinesthetic motoric learners, who look for every opportunity to move about in the classroom. In addition, because they enjoy this, they are often very good at miming.

h) This appeals mostly to kinesthetic motoric learners because they like things they can touch and move about, and visual learners, who can read the words or look at the pictures on the cards.

i) This appeals mostly to global learners because they prefer to have an overview rather than the details.

j) This appeals to auditory learners, who enjoy speaking and listening, and also to analytic learners, who like to find ways to describe things accurately.

k) This appeals to kinesthetic emotional learners, who enjoy working together with others, and also to global learners, who value teamwork and reaching goals together.

l) This appeals to global learners, who like the chance to use their own words to complete sentences, and also to kinesthetic emotional learners, who like personalized learning experiences.

2 Commentary (p. 10/11)

Task 2A
Sensory-based perception
Visual: 2, 6, 10
Auditory: 1, 3, 8
Kinesthetic motoric: 4, 9, 12
Kinesthetic emotional: 5, 7, 11

Characteristics

- *Visual* learners like to see things written down and usually take notes in class. They tend to remember where they have seen something, and might use highlighters or different colors to mark their texts. They value illustrated or colorful learning materials.
- *Auditory* learners like to listen or speak in order to remember material. They might not take notes in class because they prefer to concentrate on listening. They generally learn sequentially from the beginning to the end. They value good quality audio materials and the chance to speak in class.
- *Kinesthetic emotional* learners like to feel comfortable in groups. They generally try to connect material they need to learn with a positive experience, and learning may be very personal for them. They value understanding and the chance to express their feelings and wishes.
- *Kinesthetic motoric* learners like to try things out for themselves. They generally enjoy manipulatives that they can touch or move around, or other activities in which they can move or touch something. They value a lively classroom and the chance to engage in physical movement in class.

Task 2B
Cognitive processing
    Global: 1, 2, 4, 8
    Analytic: 3, 5, 6, 7

Characteristics
- *Global* learners process information holistically and often remember an entire experience rather than the details. They are usually relationship-oriented when working in groups and may be extrinsically motivated, as they are strongly affected by their environments. They often value feelings over facts.
- *Analytic* learners process information in a detailed and structured manner. They often remember specifics rather than the whole picture and tend to be task-oriented when doing group work. They generally value facts over feelings.

3 Commentary (p. 12)

Task 3

1. *False.* Learners often learn to adapt their learning preferences, especially if their goals cannot be reached by using the methods they are most comfortable with. This is called *stretching out of their comfort zone.*

2. *True* (up to a point). Learners may feel more comfortable when they are in stressful situations if the material they need to learn is presented in the way they best perceive and process it. However, in situations where they are feeling more relaxed and confident, they can develop strategies to learn using different methods.

3. *True.* Teachers can help learners to expand their capabilities by recognizing their basic needs. Once those needs are met, it is generally easier to help learners try out new approaches and strategies.

4. *False* (for the most part). Some things are easier to learn if your learning preference and what needs to be learned are a match. An auditory learner will probably memorize a speech more easily than a visual learner, for example; but learning preferences are not an indication of how *well* people can learn, just what comes more naturally to them.

5. *False.* Learning preferences per see have no effect on how competent someone is.

6. *True.* This is similar to the answer in 4. Some people will learn some things more easily than others simply because what they need to learn or how it is presented matches their learner type..

7. *True.* Learners often do not know what they need to help them learn, especially if they have been told that doing what came naturally was not helping them or even wrong. Experimenting with different ideas and approaches can help learners to develop the strategies they need.

8. *False.* Teachers can use the information about learner types to understand their learners and to find ways to expand their teaching styles. They are not intended to be used to categorize learners.

9. *False*. Learner types are only limiting if the individual sees them in that way. As mentioned earlier, some things come more easily to some learners than to others, but once learners are comfortable with their learning preferences, this can help them to develop self-confidence – which can encourage them to try out new strategies and ideas for themselves.

10. *False*. Learners need to understand that they cannot rely on their learning preferences to 'get out of' doing something that may be difficult for them. Having information about their learner types should help them to capitalize on their strengths and learn how to cope with the areas that are more difficult for them.

11 Commentary (p. 57)

Task 4

Example for visual learners
Predictions based on pictures appeal to visual learners because they are stimulated by images. They like looking at them, and find that pictures help them to remember vocabulary.

Example for auditory learners
Writing based on oral input is appealing to auditory learners because they remember what they hear. They then have the chance to transfer it into a written form, and find it helpful to combine these two into one exercise.

Example for kinesthetic emotional learners
Writing based on personal experiences helps kinesthetic learners relate to work they need to do. Rather than remember facts, they can access their own feelings and emotions and write about them.

Example for kinesthetic motoric learners
Acting out dialogues helps kinesthetic motoric learners combine movement with vocabulary, making it easier for them to remember the vocabulary later.

Example for global learners
Putting paragraphs in the correct order appeals to global learners because they like to see the entire picture and understand the gist of a text.

Example for analytic learners
Multiple choice comprehension questions appeal to analytic learners because they need to use logic to decide which questions are distractors and which ones are based on information in the text.

Task 5

Regarding stretching strategies, there are no specific answers here. Any strategy that is not generally used by the learner or specified in the original task could be regarded as stretching. For example, a spoken task could then be written out for homework; or a written task could be changed into a presentation. It is necessary to see how well tasks can be extended and what the logical way is to do this. Very often homework can be used to help learners stretch by adding another sensory-based channel or adding analytic or global elements to tasks designed for the other type of learner.

To become proficient at creating tasks, we need to practice. Looking back at the descriptions for different learner types and strategies, ideas for activities for different types, information on instructions, and the goals of the activities should give you enough information to try this out yourself.

12 Commentary (p. 58)

Task 7 Part 1
    Visual: *view, look at, picture, read, see, draw*
    Auditory: t*ell, describe, listen, ask, speak, dialogue, discuss, conversation*
    Kinesthetic Emotional: *agree, join, feel, support*
    Kinesthetic Motoric: *stress, touch, act out, draw*

Task 7 Part 2

1. Sensory-based language: *look at.* This is designed for visual and analytic learners and has them look at the details that help them to learn.

2. Sensory-based language: *listen, tell, discuss.* This is designed for auditory learners because they use both active and passive oral skills. It may also appeal to global learners, it asks for general topics and not details.

3. Sensory-based language: *read, conversation, agree.* This is designed for visual, auditory, and kinesthetic emotional learners because it involves reading about auditory strategies, interpersonal relationships, and agreement. It may also appeal to global learners, and talking about strategies could also be interesting for analytic learners.

4. Sensory-based language: *read, look for.* This is designed for visual and analytic learners. They are instructed to read and then need to use details to slot in the correct sentences by using logic to discover cohesion.

5. Sensory-based language: *describe, draw.* This is designed for visual, auditory, and kinesthetic motoric learners because they need to describe a drawing, listen for details, and draw, which is an activity combining visual and kinesthetic skills. Depending on the picture (serious or funny), it could appeal to most of the other types as well. As the instructions are left fairly free, other learner types normally find a way to carry out the activity using the strategies they are most comfortable with.

6. Sensory-based language. *Listen.* This is designed for auditory and analytic learners because they have to use listening skills as well as logical or analytic ones.
7. Sensory-based language: *act out.* This is designed for kinesthetic motoric learners because they are instructed to move. It also appeals to global learners because they may look for a way to demonstrate the activities in a unique manner.

13 Commentary on Task 8 (p. 60)

Collocations gapped text

This activity appeals to the kinesthetic motoric learners because they have to move cards around to complete the task. It also appeals to the analytic learners because they need to carefully consider which words are needed in the gaps. It includes an auditory element as they generally read the sentences aloud when working in groups and a visual one as the cards are marked with symbols indicating the beginning and end of the collocation. In addition, they work collaboratively which appeals to the kinesthetic emotional and global learners.

Sentence Auction

This is an analytic task as it deals with error correction. However, the groups also have to read the sentences aloud and discuss the correcting, which brings in the auditory element. It is also visual because they need to carefully read the sentences. There is an emotional kinesthetic and global factor as well because the group works together as a team to win points.

All about Me

This activity was inspired by Jill Hadfield, and is used to create empathy for another person, making it a kinesthetic emotional and global exercise. Learners imagine they are someone else and try to complete sentences. They also need to use their visual and auditory channels to discuss this at the end. Having the learners write a short story as homework brings in the analytical element because they need to make the transition from first person to third person singular, a grammar point which can be challenging for beginners and lower intermediate students.

Points to consider

Look back at these three activities and think about how they could be adapted. Could they be used for different learner types? What would need to be changed?

14 Commentary on Task 9 (p. 63)

Part 1

    a) Visual and analytic learners

    b) Auditory and analytic learners

    c) Visual and global learners

    d) Visual, analytic, and global learners

    e) Auditory and global learners

    f) Visual and analytic learners

    g) Visual and analytic learners

    h) Visual, kinesthetic emotional, and global learners

    i) Visual and global learners

    j) Visual, kinesthetic emotional, and global learners

    k) Auditory, visual, and global learners

Note: These activity types can appeal to different learner types as well, depending on the particular language being practiced. If texts are factual, they will appeal more to analytic types; whereas if they are more personal, they will attract global and kinesthetic emotional learners.

Part 2

Design several self-study exercises for different learner types. Use some of the ideas you have come across in this module.

Try them out with your learners and get feedback from them. Find out how they reacted to the tasks you gave them and ask them which tasks helped them to understand concepts or remember material better and why. Find out what is was about a particular task that was useful or helpful for the students. This can be done as class interviews (either you interviewing the students or the students interviewing each other) or as a piece of writing in the form of a learning journal or diary.

Printed in Great Britain
by Amazon

51444853R00047